MEET THE AUTHOR

Born on January 10, 1980, this Capricorn is true to her sign. She is an ambitious, hard working author that just finished her first book, Peek Into Our Windows, which is inspired by her love for her son, who was diagnosed with Autism Spectrum Disorder in early 2008. Shaundra is a wife and mother of two children. She was raised in East Point, Georgia in a low-middle income household where education was a top priority although her parents only had high school educations. Being the youngest of four children, Shaundra looked up to her older sisters for guidance, especially after losing her mother at the young age of 17. This was a devastating loss and while she was unsure of what the future would hold, she pressed forward, finishing high school and then college. After two years of wondering what to do next, Shaundra realized that her business degree was not her passion and thus went to pursue her true passion, which was education. Since that time she has successfully taught students in special education and general education classrooms and served as an Instructional Coach in the metropolitan Atlanta area. She married her fiancé in August of 2007 and they had two children, Jeremy Christian Boyd on March 1, 2006 and Morgan Ashley Boyd on March 26, 2008. In November 2013, Shaundra was inspired to write this book and the rest is history.

Dedication...

This book is dedicated to my son, Jeremy Christian Boyd, who has inspired me to be the best mother, provider, advocate, educator, and PERSON I can be...

To my Lesley University instructor who told me that this would be my destiny even before I knew it was...

And to the late Donnie and Catherine Dodson, who instilled the work ethic, drive, and motivation in me to be the ABSOLUTE BEST at EVERYTHING. It is because of them that I AM WHO I AM!

The Author's Story

Table of Contents

Chapter I
An Introduction
page 5

Chapter II
The Beginning
page 10

Chapter III
The Diagnosis
page 20

Chapter IV
After the Diagnosis
page 27

Chapter V
A Deviation in the Plan
page 33

Chapter VI
Public School System Transition
page 38

Chapter VII
Making that Critical Decision
page 52

Chapter VIII
Life Today
Page 56

CHAPTER I
An Introduction
The Author's Story...The Boyd Clan

No one ever wants to believe that it could be their child, but one day you wake up and you come to the realization that there is something uniquely different about your son/daughter that makes him/her stand out from other children in the room. I knew that I was one of the fortunate ONES to be in the education profession, which means I held the knowledge to see the critical signs early for my son Christian. I am not, however, oblivious enough to think that in my community where low and middle income families lack the knowledge, resources, and income available to be in **" THE KNOW"**, there are many of us that have no clue what we are seeing as we watch our child change right before our eyes with developmental delays that lead to a disability that is profound yet unique beyond belief.

We call my son Christian, by his middle name, but his complete name is Jeremy Christian Boyd. As I am beginning to write this first chapter at 10:54 p.m. on November 18, 2013, he is 7 years old, living with the disability known as Autism

Spectrum Disorder. To us, he is our genius in the making. He is and will continue to defy odds and turn heads, and he has a smile that is electrifying and will win you over. He is an awesome kid, but our road hasn't been easy and it never will be, but that's the path that has been laid out for us. To others who don't know him and have no concept about what this disability is often look at him in disbelief. While it is frustrating at times to continue to try to explain to people what this disability is and how it affects him, our son has made strides that many could never fathom and each accomplishment is more rewarding than the last. The fact of the matter is that this is **Our Family, our Struggle, our Son, our World and We are Embracing IT…100%**

    Our journey began around October 2007 and when I realized what was happening, I have to admit that I briefly questioned what God was doing in my life and I cried. I asked for clarification and guidance. I asked God, "Why me, why our family, why my son, and what do we do now?" I never imagined that this would be our reality; besides no one ever plans this to be a part of his or her white picket fence life. I have never said that out loud before, but it was a true and a real emotion that I felt, and what so many other mothers and fathers feel that have been or are in this same position, but WE are only human. I now realize that God's purpose for placing this beautiful creation in our life was to make a significance difference, not just in his life, but in the lives of many others too. That still doesn't mean this road has been easy, because I promise you *each day is a struggle and a triumph rolled in one, but I wouldn't trade it now for anything.* Who else can really profess that about something so challenging? Who would really say that a task that often times has the ability to mentally, emotionally, and sometimes physically beat you down at times, is also the one true thing in your life that you hold as your HIGHEST accomplishment; that is something truly PROFOUND. Who knew that a disability, a word that has such a negative connotation to so many, can also have such a PROFOUND impact and be the **TRIUMPHANT** elephant in the room that makes you stand up tall and proclaim **I AM HERE; NOTICE ME, CHALLENGE ME, and NEVER FORGET WHO I AM, WHY I AM, and THAT I AM…SOMEBODY!** This is Jeremy Christian Boyd and the millions of other unsung hero's that live with the disability of Autism Spectrum Disorder, but this is also their parent's too.

The parents have a story they want to share. I want to tell you what our life has been like. People deserve to know what trials we have been through, what this disability is and how it affects the lives of so many Americans on a daily basis. People should know how our family and other families have persevered regardless of how hard this road has been. For these few pages we want to shed light on the medical communities reception to this disability, the educational systems response or lack thereof to adequate preparation of teachers in the public school system that teach our children, and how we have handled it all. We stay up sleepless nights and battle tantrums, and cry tears, smile when our children make strides that some parents take for granted, and then we sit back and wonder what happens next because for children with Autism, rarely does anything remain the same.

I know often times you may see the celebrities that have the ability to try alternative or unorthodox methods to help their children progress in unimaginable ways, but that isn't who we are. This book reflects the low or middle class families that don't have the overflowing pockets to support anything but the basics. In fact, we often times barely have the insurance coverage or money to pay for co-payments for doctors visits, prescriptions, or to pay for extra physical therapy, occupational therapy, and/or speech therapy that insurance doesn't pay for to push our children harder and harder towards attaining their goals, but we still fight this fight daily and we do it with dignity and honor.

    Today is the day that our stories will be shared with the world. Today is the day that we empower our community with knowledge, influence, and the ability to make progressive change. This is the beginning of a movement towards a better understanding of a disability that is changing lives and it is time for the SILENT VOICES to be HEARD AROUND THE WORLD.

Chapter II
The Beginning
The Author's Story...The Boyd Clan

My fiancé and I became pregnant in the summer of 2005 and were excited to begin this journey to parenthood as we had been together since 1997 and both would be first time parents to what we would later find out to be a baby boy. My future husband was elated and had so many plans for he and his son. Because he was a former athlete, he had already made up in his mind that his son would be also and he would be right by his side coaching him up to be a football and baseball player as he was. I was so excited to see him so excited about the birth of our son and it was a happy time for us.

My pregnancy was considered high risk because I was over weight and had hypertension and therefore I saw both a regular obstetrician/gynecologist as well as a specialist over the course of my pregnancy to eliminate or lessen complications. During this time I took medication for hypertension and went to every doctor's appointment to make sure our son would be healthy upon his arrival.

I was working as a special education teacher in a metropolitan Atlanta school district that will remain nameless for confidentiality reasons. I served a large group of special needs students as a resource and inclusion teacher, which means that students were taught in my own classroom and I also traveled to a classroom where the regular education teacher was the primary teacher and I supported instruction for the special needs students in her homeroom class. This was my second year in this position and I found it to be a breeze to work in this position because the administrators were supportive, the staff was like a family, and I had a knack for differentiated instruction and classroom management.

One day, after telling a close friend of mine about my pending pregnancy, I vividly remember a conversation we briefly had that still sticks in my mind. "Don't work around those special needs children while you're pregnant," she told me. I recall looking at her with a look of dismay, almost hoping that she was joking and then when realizing she wasn't, I asked her why. She glanced at me ever so seriously and said, "Because your child will come out like one of them." "One of them," I thought to myself. That was not only a discriminatory statement but reeked of disgust and ignorance and I was utterly surprised to hear this coming from someone I was extremely close to. I thought to myself, do people really feel this way? I would soon come to learn the harsh reality, through my own life experiences, that some people really do.

This conversation resonates so vividly in my mind because I think back to this time often now that I am living with a son that has a disability that still has no real known cause. I know it sounds foolish to the average person but for parents of children on the Autism Spectrum, we wonder why everyday. We wonder what caused this disability and because the medical community has no definitive answer to this question, anything in our mind is a possibility. The fact, however, that I am more knowledgeable about the disability, I know that it is not at all likely that my son was diagnosed with ASD because children with mild learning and behavioral disabilities surrounded me during the duration of my pregnancy with him. Her comment while it is far-fetched and ignorant to say the least, is a thought in the minds of many Americans and validates the idea that people really have no clue what ASD is, what living and parenting a child with ASD is like; thus confirms a primary reason I am here embarking on this journey to write this book today.

What seemed to be a long hard road to the delivery of my baby boy lasted 37 weeks and ended with an emergency Caesarean section, resulting in a healthy, 7 lb. 8 oz. baby boy. Over the next few months we adjusted to being new parents and lived a normal new parent life, with our son, growing and changing each day. Christian was a very happy infant, and according to the developmental charts that the doctors provided at each of his health check-ups, he was developing normally with the exception of his height and weight, which was always above the average percentile range for his age. He was a healthy eater and he consumed more formula than the average infant, which put a strain on our pockets. We purchased over 35 or more cans of formula a month at more than $5.50 per can, but thank GOD for some type of assistance during this very critical 8-week maternity leave period.

We ensured that our son kept all his pediatric appointments and got his immunizations according to the CDC Immunization Schedule. I was fully aware of the current medical information that was arising about immunizations and its possible connection or link to Autism Spectrum Disorder, however I was not willing to put my son's health at risk over a mere possibility that this may occur. This was speculation at its best according to medical professionals so we decided to immunize Christian, which now is a questionable decision in our minds and the minds of many other parents in the Autism community.

In August of 2007, when Christian was 17 months old, my fiancé and I tied the knot to become Mr. and Mrs. Boyd. It was a joyous occasion and a time for celebration. At this time Christian was eating a variety of baby food and Gerber recommended snacks in addition to his daily milk consumption. Then around the time Christian turned 18-19 months in age, we begin to notice changes that were extremely different and suddenly none of these foods interested him any longer. As new parents we immediately tried many different alternative food choices to try to get him to eat but nothing was working. This caused frustration for me, but we continued to try a variety of different foods over the months and years. For the next few months and then years, we noticed that he leaned toward eating soft textured foods such as mashed potatoes and grits, and that, to me, was a clear indication that there were sensory concerns that should be addressed. For educators, we notice these types of things, but for parents that are not in this profession, the red flag doesn't always exist when you see these types of issues arising.

Along with the changes in Christian's eating habits came the observable abnormalities in how he was interacting with his toys. As a parent that paid close attention to the simple things in my child, I noticed how he would play with his toy Tonka cars. Instead of rolling them across the floor, he would choose to line them up very straight across the floor. The interesting thing that came with this process of lining up the toys was also the fact that he would become very angry if anyone would come by and push the cars out of line, either intentionally or unintentionally. For a month or two it was only the toy cars that he would do this for, but then he transitioned this process to more than toys, and became obsessed with almost any like objects he could find. For example, if he could find multiple crayons or balls he would line them up in as straight a line as possible. It became intriguing and odd at the same time.

The most critical piece to the noticeable changes was the communication. My son had always maintained appropriate communication development through 2 years of age as well as eye contact during those communication exchanges. It wasn't until before his 2nd birthday that his speech development seemed to be halted and that his eye contact became limited. It was extremely odd to us as parents to see this behavior occurring because it was a rapid change that was almost here one day, and gone the next. ***It was as if we woke up one day and our son seemed so distant and removed from this world.*** I would call his name and he would no longer look me in the eye in acknowledgement. He was no longer developing new speech and in fact his speech was digressing back to almost babbling as if he was an infant again. I was now extremely confused and as a concerned, knowledgeable mom, I immediately became worried about my son's emotional, social, and physical health.

      The paradox in all of this is that it wasn't only my son's behavior, however, that I was concerned about during this very critical time. While it may sound absurd to some, I was also extremely worried about my husband's behavior at this time. My husband, in my opinion, was not as concerned about our son's behavior as I was and I was unsure why he wasn't. I asked myself was it just my husband's passive nature that caused his lack of concern or was it a true denial about not wanting to believe that there could truly be something wrong with his son; a son that he had such high hopes for? It was important for me to keep communication between us extremely open so that I could prevent something detrimental from occurring.

I had a family that was so new to me, a new husband, a new son, but in the back of my mind we were at a pivotal point where we could possibly be breaking down because of what I knew was about to happen to us. I knew what I was seeing when others couldn't see or didn't want to see. As a parent that worked as a special education teacher, I knew exactly what I was seeing unfold right before my eyes, and although I was prepared every day to accept a child to walk into my classroom with this disability and teach them and accept the challenge, I had to admit that I too was like many other parents and held that initial fear and thought that I didn't want this for my OWN child.

Before picking up the phone to call a doctor, there were a few things I needed to do in order to prepare our family for what was about to occur. I hadn't written these things out, but subconsciously, I knew that there were things that I needed to do as a mother, wife, and educator in order to get ready for this transition that was about to occur in our house and I had to do those things quickly in order to make this road a little easier for us. The first of these things were to convince myself that we were ready to take on this challenge that was about to take us head first into places unforeseen. Getting ready never means being ready, but it is merely psyching yourself out to believe that you can do this even though you are scared beyond belief that this is happening to you and realizing more that the life you had planned is about to go down a path that you can't predict. It's a scary place folks and yet you don't have a choice but to accept it and stand firm in knowing that God has your back in it all.

      Secondly, I had to have a real, honest conversation with my husband about what we were about to encounter and how it could impact the future for both our son and us. This was a difficult conversation to have with a man that not only had so many plans for his son, but one who also operates in a very passive manner that could possibly yield a reaction that I would not understand and thus result in a disagreement if not received by me in the best light. Nevertheless, I had to have the conversation and we did and although I don't think he was able to conceptualize everything that I was explaining to him about this disability at the time, he was ready and willing to accept that his son would be undergoing changes and challenges and above all he wanted to continue to be the best father and husband he could be to our family to get us through this very trying time. I was happy to say the least and proud to be a part of this new family, but still apprehensive about what was to come next.

    Lastly, I relied on my faith and prayed for guidance and understanding to do what was right for my son. While I was knowledgeable and educated, I didn't know everything and I wanted to be guided by God to make the right decisions for my child to ensure that he is always on the best path physically, emotionally, educationally, and spiritually. This was an essential piece to the puzzle for me as I closed this chapter of my life and opened up the next chapter to lead toward the diagnosis and communicating with professionals about my son's needs and my expectations for his success and progress.

Chapter III
The Diagnosis
The Author's Story…The Boyd Clan

The 2-year-old check up was the beginning of our step towards receiving an official diagnosis for Christian. We addressed our major concerns with his primary pediatrician about the things that we were observing at home, the communication deficits and behavioral and eating changes. During this visit, his pediatrician asked more in-depth questions about these things that ultimately led to a referral to an excellent developmental pediatrician. Our initial appointment was weeks out, as this doctor was extremely booked for new patient appointments. On the day of the appointment the waiting area was full of families that were anxiously waiting to see the doctor, each one anticipating what he would have to say about their child as I speculated from the looks on their faces. There was an air of nervousness from many of the parents as I observed their body language and listened to the conversations that were going on throughout the area. The diversity in the waiting room came as no surprise to me, as an individual that knows that Autism has no racial or ethnic boundaries.

We waited for what seemed to be hours and filled out loads of paperwork, which included questionnaires and family history information. Finally we entered those double doors that led to another waiting area and rooms where you could hear children that were making a variety of different sounds, some squealing, others talking, and others babbling, all of which were quite interesting to say the least. As we walked to the nurse's station to have a seat and discuss the paperwork that we had filled out in the initial waiting area, she discussed our primary concerns and our goals and expectations for our initial visit and then escorted us to the room to wait for the doctor. As we passed several other rooms, some empty, others occupied, I remember looking into each of them just to see what the children looked like inside, wondering what they would look like and how they would behave and if they had any similarities to our son. Not to my surprise, each of them looked and behaved completely different from our son and from the next individual in the room next door. That is the one really unique thing about children on the Autism Spectrum that parents, educators, and people in general have to understand. Children diagnosed with this disability are each uniquely different from the next and that in itself makes this disability one that is extremely difficult to understand. Children with Autism require specialized, individual support from those around them to ensure that they make the most progress possible.

As we finally arrived to our room and made ourselves comfortable, I found myself almost daydreaming about what the doctor would think, say, and/or recommend for our child as a result of this visit. All the "what ifs" rest in the back of my mind and there was an uneasy feeling that just wouldn't go away. As I snapped back to reality and remembered our true reason for being there on this very important day, I laid all those fears aside and became truly open to the idea that my son would leave here the same as he had come but with a diagnosis that may ***stigmatize*** him for life.

The doctor finally walked into the room and his voice and enthusiasm about getting to know our concerns about our child immediately calmed me and made me feel safe. I'm stressing my emotions because for my husband, s he was as cool as a fan and didn't seem at all, impacted by what was happening. His tough exterior seemed to be equally matched with a rigid interior and I wondered how he managed to always hold it together so well, but he does and once again on this occasion he did again. For me, however, feeling safe was important because as a concerned parent that was seeking more understanding and guidance from a medical professional, it demonstrates that the person to whom we are entrusting our sons health and happiness to is genuinely concerned about his wellbeing and health. After asking some pertinent questions and reviewing the questionnaire that we provided at the intake process, the doctor spent 10-15 additional minutes conducting an observation of our son. During the observation we noticed how intrigued even the doctor was with our son's behavior as he was lining up the toy cars. He even asked permission to videotape a portion of this part of the observation because of his interest in it and we agreed. He followed up the observation by discussing in detail with us how the diagnosis of Autism occurs. This was one of the most critical pieces of the diagnosis process that parents should be knowledgeable about because it provides insight on the areas in which children qualify for a diagnosis on the Autism Spectrum. In fact, expectant parents and new parents should be well aware of this process as well in order to be able to clearly identify some signs that may indicate that their child(ren) may need to be evaluated by a health professional (*Please refer to the DSM-V to see the revised criteria for diagnosing a child with Autism Spectrum Disorder*).

During 2008, the criteria for the diagnosis of ASD was slightly different, based on the DSM-IV at that time, nevertheless, it was clear that our son fit the conditions and by the time we left the doctor's office there was a clear diagnosis of ASD for our son. While I knew that this would already be the outcome going into this doctor's appointment, all of a sudden it became real for us and I was more nervous to walk out the door with the paperwork in our hand that proclaimed that my son was officially on the Autism Spectrum.

Our doctor provided us with recommendations for resources and next steps, which was extremely helpful. The difference between our family and many other families is that we acted on the information we received in regards to the diagnosis. There is a real reason why I made the statement above and that is because many other parents operate in a denial mindset. When a parent operates in a denial mindset this means that a few things may take place in my opinion:

1. Failure to report their concerns that they have observed at home to the pediatrician because they do not want to admit that there is a problem; thus they

will never receive a referral to the developmental pediatrician or specialist to receive a diagnosis.
2. Report the concerns they are observing at home and receive a referral to a developmental pediatrician but fail to follow up with him/her to receive a diagnosis.
3. Report the concerns to the pediatrician and receive a referral to a developmental pediatrician/specialist, follow up by attending an initial appointment, but subsequently fail to initiate services for the child in order to ensure adequate development and progress.

The problem that exists when parents choose to deny the inevitable is that the child is the one that ultimately suffers. Early intervention for children with ASD is the best way to ensure that the child can develop and progress to his/her fullest potential. However, if parents don't realize that they may be hindering their child's progression by first admitting that there is a problem and then allowing for intervention, then they are the first people in their child's life that is doing them a disservice.

Often times we, as parents, want to point the blame at others, sometimes the educational system and other times, the medical community (who will be addressed later in this book) about their failure to support and adequately help our children met and attain their goals as children with special needs. However, sometimes we also have to take an honest look in the mirror at ourselves; self-reflection is a powerful tool that helps us determine how we can become better in many aspects, even as parents. As a parent that strongly believes that WE are our child's first teachers, we are responsible for putting aside our doubts, fears, and inhibitions to ensure that we are not standing in the way of our child's development and progress. It is easy for a parent to be scared and embarrassed and to be in denial of what is right in front of them and sweep the obvious under the rug, but years down the line the child will truly be the one who will suffer from the lack of support and services that could have been provided. It is easier said than done because I know, but I also know that my son Christian would not be as successful as he is today if I had decided to close my eyes to the truth. Our truth has set us free and so will it for every other family that is in the exact same situation. Truth is a powerful thing…what you do with it will determine your destiny

Chapter IV
After the Diagnosis
The Author's Story...The Boyd Clan

The days immediately following the diagnosis weren't easy but we managed to make it through them together as a family. We were trying hard to balance work and scheduling the initial appointment for the Babies Can't Wait (BCW) Program to come out to do an initial assessment for our son. The Babies Can't Wait Program is a state funded program that provides services for infants and toddlers until age 3 that have special needs. Every state is mandated by federal law to have a program in place such as this for children with disabilities. This is pertinent information for parents to know so that they will be able to access resources in their community for their child with special needs.

Christian, at this time, was in a great childcare facility that was extremely receptive to special needs students and they worked hard to accommodate his needs as a student in the classroom. It is extremely important to a parent to find a facility that is open and willing to accept students with disabilities because some aren't always willing and don't recognize the care and responsibility that it requires to take on a child that has special needs. I was indebted to this facility for not only their willingness to support the educational progress of our child, but also for the patience, time, effort, and provision they provided to our family during this transition for our son. They went through the journey with us and it was so wonderful to have them in our life.

    The director was extremely pleasant and worked with our family closely to assist us in providing Christian with all the services necessary to help him succeed. We became like a family and she and the staff came to love him and wanted to see him progress and develop to his fullest potential. This was the ideal place for Christian to be during this critical time in his life because it was necessary for him to have support, nurturing, and understanding as he underwent these life-altering changes.

    We scheduled the meeting with the BCW coordinator assigned to our area and we waited patiently for the date to arrive to discuss our goals and expectations for our son. It was a thorough meeting with a team of individuals (therapist, etc.) who conducted an initial evaluation of our son as well as reviewed the documentation from his doctor and then discussed in detail their service recommendations, which were followed up with tons of paperwork. The services would be provided at the local childcare facility and/or home depending on the time at which the provider and parents agreed upon. The meeting was similar to that of an IEP (Individualized Education Plan) meeting, but instead we received and IFSP, an Individual Family Service Plan. This is the document that drives the services that will be provided to our son just as the IEP drives the services and accommodations/modifications that a student will be provided in a public school system. As we wrapped up the meeting, I felt confident in the team's assessment and was interested in meeting the therapists that would be working with Christian. That would be the next step in this process. Each step of this process for me seemed to become more nerve wrecking than the next as we created a schedule and timelines to complete tasks along with trying to balance the normal occurrences of everyday life. It often times became a bit overwhelming as life sometimes does, but the Capricorn woman in me never backs down from a challenge and with the Leo husband of mine always remaining calm, cool, and collected and standing as strong as a mighty Lion, it was clear that we could take on the world, no matter how hard the task was.

We were contacted by each of the therapist separately and scheduled a time to meet with each of them to discuss the scheduling of services. It was an opportunity to discuss our expectations with professionals and the beginning of the intervention of services for our son. The coordination of these services were in place and began by the time Christian was 30 months and I think this has significantly contributed to his success thus far. The longer the wait to receive services, the more time that passes that your child may have received some specific skills and learning that would have impacted their understanding of a specific concept. These trained professionals have the skills and knowledge to help students with various disabilities become successful, and we as parents have an obligation to ensure that we provide our children with the resources that will allow them to succeed as much as possible.

While I understand that in my community that it may not seem that simple to get through this process, especially for mothers who may be juggling more than one child or job, or may be a single mother who lacks help and support from family members, but I beg to differ and others do as well. You'll see why as you read the other powerful stories included in this book. The bottom line lies in the fact that all your children deserve an equal amount of your love, attention, and time. As you would devote the time to take one child to the doctor because they were sick from an illness, so is it your obligation to take your child to the doctor if they are displaying symptoms of delayed developmental issues. And that prescription that you faithfully take to the local pharmacy and fill for your "normal" child for antibiotics is equal to the recommendation of services for your child with developmental delays and should not be ignored, but should also be filled by the professionals that are required to ensure developmental progress can be made. Mothers of all children hold an obligation to their children to ensure that they have everything they need to be healthy physically, emotionally, and developmentally!

    For the remainder of his months as a 2 year old, Christian received his occupational and speech services through the BCW program at the childcare facility and at home. It was the ideal situation because it provided the childcare facility with an opportunity to acquire additional resources and support needed to care for our son, as well as, for future enrollees that may need assistance in the future.

Additionally, providing services in our home, also gave us the opportunity to see the professional at work and Christian's level of engagement with her, the techniques and activities she utilized with him, and the progress he was or was not making over time. It was a great opportunity to be involved in his intervention and as parents of children, you should, as much as possible be involved in this process. Regardless of the fact that I am an educator, I am not all knowing and can still learn from others and continue to do so every chance I get. It is incumbent upon you to take the initiative to involve yourself in the process of learning what it is that you don't know. Ignorance is not an excuse, which is yet another reason for my writing this book. Your opportunity to learn and grow will come from reading, understanding, and asking the right questions of the right people.

As Christian approached his 3rd birthday, the BCW program would soon come to a close (remember earlier I stated that this program was from infancy to age 3) and he would be transitioning to a new phase that would bring on a whole new world of challenges.

Chapter V
A Deviation in the Plan
The Author's Story...The Boyd Clan

Flashback to the summer of 2007, during the time when we were scheduling and waiting for appointments to get services scheduled for the BCW program for Christian. At the same exact time, I had begun to feel sick and nauseated and wasn't at all up to getting out the bed on some days to do anything. Unfortunately being a mother and wife is a 24-hour job and there is never a dull moment, for mothers of children on the Autism Spectrum. It was starting to wear on me, and as a person who goes to see the doctor for any and everything (I think I am OCD for this), I went in to see what was wrong, and much to my surprise, I found out that we were having yet another baby.

A wave of emotions all came down on me at one time. I was happy, sad, nervous, and scared all at once. I felt these flow of emotions that I know many mothers feel because this wasn't at all a planned pregnancy, but I also know that mothers of children with Autism share these emotions for other reasons. For some mothers, it is a scary emotion to wonder if you will carry yet another child that will have the same disability. You wonder will my life be twice as stressful or is there anything I can do differently to ensure that this child is not impacted by this disability? I left the doctor's office with a wave of emotions and knowing that I had to tell my husband this news and not knowing what he may feel about it as well. As I entered the house and sat him down to let him in on the information that would change our lives yet again, surprisingly he was not as surprised as I was to hear the news and was excited that we were expecting. I guess I shouldn't have been shocked by his response since he had always talked about wanting plenty of kids. I initially was on board with that idea, until we were faced with the challenge of raising a child with Autism and my outlook on that idea shifted a little, but for him it obviously had not. Nevertheless, the addition to the family was clearly a deviation from my plan but not from God's plan. Once again I accepted what God was doing in my life and no matter how nervous and worried I was, I went trusted and had faith that everything would be fine.

    For the next 9 months, as my pregnancy had been with Christian, I was nauseated and exhausted, suffering from high blood pressure, and at now my heaviest weight ever. None of that stopped me, however, from putting all my time and effort into Christian. I was not sure how the addition of Morgan would impact our household and Christian's behavior. I wondered how he would receive a new addition to the family or if at his age, he even understood what was happening. I tried to take the time out to explain to him what was going on and to let him know that mommy and daddy were having a new baby. Whether or not he fully understood our conversations and all the times I allowed him to feel the kicks in my stomach still remains a mystery. What I do know is that on March 26, 2008, our new precious bundle of joy arrived and we were excited to have her in our lives. This time we were able to prepare for the arrival of our new bundle of joy since Morgan was a planned cesarean that went off with no complications.

My days in the hospital after delivering Morgan were up and down because Christian was not able to be there with us throughout the nights. By this time he was far more active, but in unfamiliar places, extremely apprehensive, so for his time in the hospital while Morgan was just born, my husband left at nights to stay with Christian at home. That is the nature of how things are sometimes in our family; one parent has to focus one child and the other focus on the other because at times that is the only way to balance things out. I wish that our family could've stayed altogether at the hospital during Morgan's first days, or on several other occasions as well, but unfortunately those are the adjustments we have to make and we do so for the betterment of our family.

    Over the next days and weeks, Christian was getting adjusted to Morgan's arrival. He would look over in the crib almost in amazement at her and when she would cry he would be slightly irritated but would come to my side to look at her, in a very protective way, to ensure that I was comforting her. He was definitely a big brother and as time continued on he was adjusting to having a new addition to the family. It was for us however, a very trying time to juggle these two children, both very needy. When my husband was back at work, I was at home juggling everything while still out on maternity leave and I was feeling overwhelmed, exhausted, and frustrated at times. In the midst of all the turmoil, and frustration I sometimes felt, when nighttime fell upon me, I was still able to lie down and look at our beautiful creations, and the many wonderful blessings that God had bestowed upon us, and be thankful.

Clearly, in my eyes this was a deviation from my plan, but God always has a way of showing you that your way is not always **THE WAY**. It has truly been a blessing to have Morgan in our lives because she is a genius too, articulate and vocal, and she has helped to make Christian more outgoing and social and she works daily with him to ensure he meets his educational gains as well. Christian, in turn, has helped Morgan understand the importance of diversity, love, and compassion and those are by far, some of life's most valuable lessons.

It is so true that God knows what you need before you really need it, and Morgan Ashley Boyd is living proof of that. While it wasn't our plan to have her only two years after Christian, God understood that it was necessary to place her here in this family at that specific time to fulfill some very specific purposes and we are grateful. Never underestimate why things happen in your life. God has truly revealed things to me but I had to be open enough to receive what he was saying. Once I allowed myself to do that, only then was I truly able to understand why and also never to question it.

Chapter VI
Public School System Transition
The Author's Story...The Boyd Clan

  The transition to the public school was seamless when Christian turned 3 years old. It was the beginning of a new world for our son as he would be entering a new arena for receiving educational services that would be exciting for him and bring new challenges for us and for his childcare providers. I was excited for what was in store for him because I knew that with the right educators and support staff in place, my son would soar, and we were adamant that he did. As we were meeting to discuss the plan for his transition, I was hopeful that the school would be adequate in implementing the goals set forth for the upcoming school year and because the school was extremely close to our house, it gave my husband the opportunity to stop by when the opportunity presented itself to drop in from time to time. With this half-day schedule, Christian was dropped off to his daycare facility at 11:30 a.m., where he would complete the afternoon until I could pick him up after work.

  This schedule was a great transition and came at the appropriate age for Christian. At 3 years old, it allowed him the opportunity to get accustomed to the structure necessary for formal schooling and because he had an outstanding teacher that was dedicated to ensuring the needs of her students were met daily, his progress was wonderful. She was young and ambitious and she kept in constant communication with us. She exemplified what all true educators, especially special education teachers, should be, and I appreciated her for the hard work and commitment she displayed everyday. At the daycare center, however things were becoming a tad bit more frustrating for Christian. As he was beginning to become accustomed to the structure and focus of the classroom of the public school system, things became a little confusing for him at the childcare facility and his behavior was beginning to become more hyperactive and less manageable for the staff to control.

    At this time, Christian was not on any medication and that was a very critical decision my husband and I made together. We were not willing to medicate our son until we felt that it was absolutely necessary, besides that is a SERIOUS decision that should not be made hastily. As an educator, I was on the fence about medication because I had seen some of my own students have adverse effects from prescribed medications but I also knew that their conditions possibly warranted the need for some of those medications as well. For my son, at this age, we did not see the need yet to consider this as an option, although he had begun to exhibit a little hyperactive behavior. The childcare director and teacher were still as patient as ever with working with him and we embraced her for that because it was so hard to find facilities that had staff that were trained and that WE could entrust with our precious SON. As the months passed for his first partial academic school year in the public school setting, I was satisfied with the outcome and progress that was made in the public education school system. I was ready to continue to move forward and for Christian to make continued progress towards becoming the very bright, intelligent student that he would be.

  Christian continued to visit his developmental pediatrician for follow up visits to check on his academic and overall developmental progress. It was always great to see his doctor and to discuss his progress and how he had grown over time. The one thing I truly loved about him was that he never forced the issue of medication. This was so important to us not only because of our opposition to it, but also because I think that parent's should know that there are other alternatives to consider first. As Christian closed out his first year in the public school system, we still battled challenges in regards to speech development, food intake, and fine motor skills, thus his developmental pediatrician referred us to a place to provide him more specialized services for children specifically on the Autism Spectrum called the Marcus Autism Center. While I was already familiar with this facility, we were still excited for our son to be seen by a specialist at this location. The time was bittersweet, because of the great relationship we had developed with his doctor but we were ready to open this new chapter in a great place where the reputation was wonderful for treating children that were just like our son.

As we prepared to enter the Pre-Kindergarten year, which would be the first full academic year for Christian in the public school system, we were excited that he would be participating in a great program for SDD (Significantly Developmentally Delayed) students in South Fulton County where he would be receiving his same services under yet another outstanding teacher that was phenomenal with working with students with ASD. I was, at this time, extremely pleased with the school systems response to their preparation of educators in the special needs classrooms in this county because they were, up until this point, adequately prepared to meet the needs of my child. By age 4, Christian was more active, but when engaged in quality, rigorous classroom activities, he was a great student that was manageable and enjoyed schooling.

By this time, however, we had relocated to a new home and it was difficult to find a new childcare facility that specialized in working with children on the Autism Spectrum. My husband had a more flexible schedule than I, working in the hospitality industry, and therefore he had to coordinate changes to ensure that he was available for the transportation drop off everyday when our son was released from school. This was a strain on his work schedule as well as a financial strain on our household but we did what needed to be done for Christian. When layoffs occurred at his job however, he was one of the first to be cut but nothing ever deterred us from ensuring that our children had the best that we could provide and we continued to move forward, supporting one another through the trying times, although times got extremely rough and frustrating at times.

During this academic school year, we began to go to the Marcus Autism Center to discuss Christian's growing hyperactivity challenges and a few new issues that were becoming serious concerns for our household. The appointments for most professionals that work with children diagnosed with ASD require waits that are months away and this office visit was no different. Nevertheless, the wait was well worth it as we were able to sit and converse with an extremely knowledgeable professional about issues that impacted our household in significant ways. Our primary concern was the fact that Christian had now started waking up in the middle of the night, usually around 1:00 a.m. and would remain awake or would fall back asleep right before it was time to get ready for school. This was an extremely tiring experience because this meant that my husband or I would have to remain up with him each night this would happen and still manage to go on with our normal duties for the day. However we would be exhausted and sleep deprived and so would Christian; which would result in more aggressive behavior for him at school. It was becoming intolerable for everyone involved and we needed answers quickly before we all became too exhausted to function normally in our everyday lives. The doctor informed us to try first a non-medication option, Melatonin, first, to see if this would help our son before trying any other possibility.

In regards to his increased hyperactive behavior our discussion led to a decision not to prescribe any medication at that time. We also received referrals to the feeding clinic and the in house social worker to receive resources in regards to toileting and potty training. Because Christian was 4 years old and still struggling in this area, this was an extremely important concern for us because I wanted my son to attain all the necessary life skills to function normally in society. This was an immediate goal for us and I worked aggressively with him and the school to ensure that we were on the same page to get him potty trained as soon as possible.

Overall our first appointment at the Marcus Autism Center was a success and we implemented the recommendations suggested. In the upcoming weeks we would follow up with the doctor to discuss the outcomes of those recommendations. The lack of sleep throughout the night continued while instituting the non-medication recommendation, which means our life was yet again in turmoil, and our stress and frustration level was at an all time high. This was one of the most critical times in our marriage and I was almost at my breaking point. We were always on edge and argued consistently about who was next to stay up, who was more tired, and so much more. It honestly scared me to think that my precious baby could be the reason to cause a separation between us. The reality of the situation is that many relationships, when children are diagnosed with ASD, fail to survive because of the stress that parents endure on a daily basis.

    The teachers saw a change in Christian's behavior because he was tired when he came to school. He was sleep deprived and with the hyperactivity already being an issue, aggressive behaviors arose. We returned back to the doctor to discuss the results of the first option, which had no effect on his sleeping pattern. This time the recommendation was to put him on a small dosage of Clonidine, which is a blood pressure lowering medication that will induce sleep; thus resulting in a full 8-9 hour night's sleep. Our hope was that with this full nights rest that Christian's hyperactive and aggressive behavior would subside and the need to consider medication to control these behaviors would be a distant memory. We agreed with the plan and we were excited to hopefully get a full nights rest, something we hadn't seen in a very long time. After about a week of introducing the new medication, we saw a significant change in Christian's sleeping pattern and we were excited that he was able to get a full night's rest. When he awoke in the morning he was ready to start the school day without any interruptions. The teachers stated that they noticed a significant change in the aggression but not necessarily in the hyperactivity that he displayed. However, they felt that within the classroom he was progressing well because they included structured activities daily and were on solid routines that made a significant difference. It was important that any environment that Christian was involved in provided routines and procedures because if not, he would be extremely over stimulated and hyperactive.

The Pre-Kindergarten year, although we experienced a few roadblocks, was a good year for his continued transition into the school system and we were once again satisfied with the school systems response to educating our child this academic school year. The staff was knowledgeable, compassionate, and SERIOUS about the job they had set forth to do. The IEP meeting at the close of this school year was more interesting than the last as they told us they would be placing Christian in a Discrete Trials Unit for ASD students. To help you better understand about Christian's Kindergarten year, I want to provide you specific information about discrete trials and what it is to provide you with clear information on what lead to my extreme displeasure with the school system on this particular school year. According to Bogin, Sullivan, Rogers, & Stabel (2010), "Discrete trial training (DTT) is a method of teaching in which the adult uses adult- directed, massed trial instruction, reinforcers chosen for their strength, and clear contingencies and repetition to teach new skills (1)". To interpret this in lamest terms, means that the adult teacher conducts trials with the students based on the individual goals set for the student and through repetition and clear expectations, the students should achieve mastery of the goals over time. Objectives that involve fine and gross motor skills, recreation, self-care, cognitive, and academic skills are very often appropriate for DTT according to Bogin et al. (2010). After researching this method I was satisfied with allowing Christian to participate in this type of unit for his Kindergarten year because I was well aware of the structure that it would provide and that we could focus on specific academic, life skills, and behavioral goals that we would like to accomplish and then collect data to ensure that it would be accomplished.

Once again I was excited about what was in store for Christian, but this new discrete trials unit was not at the same school, so again he was transitioning to a new school across town, and being introduced to a new teacher. I was hoping that this new educator was as excited, ambitious, and knowledgeable as the two previous ones that we had encountered, but being an educator myself, I also know that every educator is built the same. With that in mind, I started his Kindergarten school year off optimistic, like I had the past school years, but still knowing in the back of my mind what possibilities could lie ahead. It didn't take long for me to see what was in store for this school year after meeting his teacher, and to say the least I was an unhappy parent that the administrators at the school and downtown level heard from on many occasions. The educator was new to the special education classroom and it was evident, and while I have been a new special education teacher once before, I engulfed myself in learning and understanding and researching to ensure I gave my student's my BEST everyday. I don't expect any less from any other new or old educator, especially one that is serving my child. I made it clear to the school and district that I will never let my son be the guinea pig for anyone's classroom. By mid-year, I had ensured that there was instructional support in place to actively monitor to ensure that my son's IEP was being fully implemented. I ensured this was the case before additional measures would have to be taken to ensure my son's educational progress was top priority. I was disgusted by this teacher's lack of ambition and enthusiasm. I was more disgusted by the school's failure to provide him with additional training when I made it clear to them that he lacked the skills necessary to perform the job. While I am not the end all, be all, in regards to teacher preparation, I do know what adequate instruction looks like and what effective parental communication should sound like. I was disheartened by the thought that my son had to be in this classroom with an inadequate educator that wasn't ready to receive him, but the worst part about it was that I've seen this in classrooms over and over again in the districts I've worked for, but it always hits harder when it hits home.

I had several meetings, phone conferences, emails, calls downtown, and angry moments during that Kindergarten school year and needless to say, it was not a great year for us. The one good thing that is good about OUR situation is that I am an educator and so my work at home with Christian made a difference. More importantly to this story however, is that as an educator, I am able to clearly articulate my displeasure in the teacher's failure to adhere to federal, state, and/or local guidelines and policies based on data and observation, which most parents in my community cannot assert with authority. KNOWLEDGE is absolutely necessary for every parent, but for a parent of a child with any disability, I URGE YOU to educate yourself 1000 times more so that you can ASSERT to anyone what is taking place or not taking place in your child's classroom. If something isn't adequate in regards to instruction, implementation of IEP goals/objectives, etc., then YOU should be able to articulate what adjustments need to be made. These adjustments should not be based on opinions either but rather on facts, according to the federal guidelines and policies outlined by IDEA. It is just that simple. We have to do it for our children because if we don't, who will. That requires more time and our attendance at IEP meetings. It requires research and getting involved in groups that will teach you what you need to know so that you can clearly communicate with the school system personnel. It isn't hard but it does require more and you must be willing to take that extra minute, hour, day, and/or week. It makes the difference and it forces the hand of the school system to say, "we can't shortchange this child". Imagine then if every parent came with that type of ammunition (the KNOWLEDGE of being in "THE KNOW" instead of "NOT KNOWING"), then we now put the school system at a disadvantage unless they are willing to serve every child with an IEP APPROPRIATELY. Shortchanging a child with any disability could never be an option again………..IMAGINE THAT!!!!

We ended the year with high hopes for the upcoming year and I adamantly demanded that Christian be moved to an alternate location with a more qualified teacher who would utilize more assistive technology considering he was still non-verbal yet his receptive communication was at or right below age appropriateness. The public school year transition was beginning to take unexpected turns but it wasn't anything we couldn't and didn't handle. More changes came but they would be changes that would prove to restore our faith in this school system.

Chapter VII
Making THAT Critical Decision
The Author's Story…The Boyd Clan

After the end of a troubling school year for Christian, we continued to observe an increase in his hyperactive behavior. While we were well aware that part of this was a direct result of the unstructured classroom environment that he was a part of during his Kindergarten year, we also knew that his ability to control his impulsive tendencies were becoming harder for him to manage. My husband and I sat down and had a serious conversation about this very important decision in regards to even considering medication because both of us, up until this point had completely opposed the idea, but once again I had to put my educator hat on. Our ultimate goal is to ensure that our son can develop and progress and achieve the highest goals possible as a child on the Autism Spectrum. I never wanted to allow him to feel slighted in regards to what he was able to achieve because he couldn't control his impulses or focus or attend to a particular task in order to get the understanding and as his parents it is our responsibility to make the right decisions to ensure that this never happens.

As an average American family that works daily and that deal with real life issues such as lay offs and having to make scheduling changes that play a role in the financial well being of our household, we are not afforded the same opportunities as the celebrities who can afford all the high end alternatives available on the market that can benefit children with ASD. The disadvantage to being "average" or "middle" income however is that we also never qualify for low-income benefits. We end up in a significantly disadvantaged situation that puts our children more at risk. Many nights I have cried, hoping and wishing that I would have the opportunity to provide my son with some of the therapeutic possibilities that exist out there for children with ASD that are not medication based, but for us, and our current situation, it isn't a possibility that we can fathom, yet I never give up hope.

After the conversation with my husband and meeting with our son's psychiatrist, we made the critical decision to finally start Christian on a small dosage of medication that would help control his hyperactive behavior. Our goal was to see an increase in his educational achievement and he has truly soared. I haven't looked back once on that decision to ensure the success of my son in the academic setting because I knew that it was warranted. I love him enough to know that sometimes I have to be objective in my decisions to ensure that Christian will grow to be the best that he can be. Isn't that what parenting is about? Parenting must be about making objective decisions that will benefit your child for years to come, but also being able to be reflective enough to know that every decision won't be perfect because no one is. However, if we do what we feel in our heart is the best for our child(ren) and if it those decisions are grounded in LOVE, then we have parented them the best we can.

  Making that key decision on that day was really hard for me, but I wasn't the only one impacted. I saw a different side to my husband that day that let me know just how important this decision was for him as well. Mr. Boyd always stood strong and never wavered, often showing little emotion, as he was definitely the calm, cool, and collected one of the two of us. On this day however, he battled with saying yes, as he read and listened to all the possible side effects, but as we talked about the implications if Christian moved forward without any help, my husband began to truly see the bigger picture. I think on this day he truly came to the realization that his future football player son was never a possibility. He broke down on this day, and I had to be the strong one and gently said to him "OUR SON will be GENIUS in many other ways, don't fret."

It is hard to realize sometimes that the hopes and dreams that we had planned while we were carrying our son will never come to fruition, but the great thing about dreams is that they have the ability to be altered. I never dreamed I would be writing this book, yet here I am finalizing the last pages to a book that is inspired by my SON who has AUTISM, but will never live a day allowing it to DEFINE WHO HE IS. Christian's dreams have been molded and shaped into something different than what we had planned, but not what GOD already had in store for HIM. It is a journey that is ultimately his to take and as parents we are ONLY charged with the great responsibility to facilitate it the best way we can.

Chapter VIII
Life Today
The Author's Story…The Boyd Clan

As Christian moved on to 1st Grade, we met a teacher that has truly become part of our family. Mrs. Curiel is truly the epitome of what every special education teacher should be. I wish that every teacher shared as much love and compassion for their students as she does because she truly made me excited to send my child to school everyday. Christian looped with Mrs. Curiel for two years and is still making significant gains to accomplish his IEP goals/objectives everyday. While I know that every teacher isn't as invested as she is, we are grateful to her for having the ambition and desire to move each and every one of her students forward so that they are truly NOT LEFT BEHIND.

While school has managed to return to a somewhat normal state, the same cannot be said for our household. Our home can sometimes be chaotic depending on Christian's mood and temperament. We continue to work with his doctor at the Marcus Autism Center to find the right dose and combination of medication to balance his aggression and hyperactivity. Some days are definitely better than others and any change in routines and procedures can make a good day a horrible one. Regardless of that fact, we work through the tantrums and highs and lows as a cohesive unit.

    Morgan has become more adjusted to understanding that her brother is different but we often find that we have to continue to remind her that there are clear differences that exist between them. This is hard for a 5 year old to understand but she works to embed the idea in her brain everyday and embraces and loves him unconditionally regardless. As she gets older, I know that she will be an advocate for disabled individuals because of the compassion and protection she shows for him now. The struggle I face when dealing with Morgan is to ensure that I don't neglect her and always make sure she feels as special as Christian does. Often times, parents can be so consumed with the special needs child that they may somewhat neglect the other child(ren); thus making them feel inadequate and/or lonely. My husband and/or I try to ensure that we make a conscious effort to include Morgan in all activities unless we are completing a specialized task that requires us to only work with Christian. In addition, we do only special activities with Morgan just so she can have that one on one time with one parent to discuss her feelings with us or just to make her feel that she is special too. It is important for her to have that validation from us now and as her parents, we feel that we are required to do this for her because they are both EQUALLY IMPORTANT TO US.

As we continue to work with both of our children at home to support their educational progress, I could only wish that we could afford the private schooling and/or other alternative methods that are available for children diagnosed with ASD. Celebrities across the nation have spoken about different therapeutic methods that have helped their children overcome many of the limitations that ASD has placed on them, but for average families like mine, we truly do not have the income to support these approaches. Without these financial resources available to us, our children, in my opinion, aren't given the same opportunities, but we are working as equally as hard for them. I am not saying that they are not justified in having what they have and providing their children what they are providing them. What I am saying is that MIDDLE CLASS families always get the short end of the stick because we never qualify for low income resources and we can never afford the HIGH end products/services that will ensure we can be on an even playing field. It is frustrating and I would be lying if I said it wasn't. But what I can tell you is that I will never stop working to ensure that my son has the best everything that is possible and that families continue to share and support one another through avenues such as this so that our voices can be heard. We are fighting a hard fight but together we will overcome the obstacles that we are faced with together. Support is crucial during times such as these.

As we plan for the future we look only at a cup that is half full because we are more knowledgeable and experienced now than we were years ago. We will utilize those experiences, along with the love and support from family members, friends, and God to guide us into a bright future that is limitless. More importantly, we know that our son, Jeremy Christian Boyd, is a brilliant young man that will continue to progress wonderfully with our support and the support of adequate educators at the school level. It is great that he has parents that are knowledgeable and involved in his education because we truly make the difference in how much he will grow and learn. It is important that other parents truly realize that they are charged with the responsibility to be actively involved in the educational process as well, regardless of whether they have a special needs child or not, because it is their duty as parents.

As an educator I have observed firsthand the impact that parental involvement makes in the classroom and while I truly do understand that it may be hard due to work schedules and other daunting tasks, sometimes we have to throw the excuses out the window and make the necessary accommodations to be there when it may count the most. I never realized that I would have to adjust my schedule so many times to take my son to his doctor appointments and to attend IEP meetings, but I haven't missed one yet, because I have made it clear to those in charge what is important to me. I am sure that if your supervisors were in the same situations they would make those adjustments to their schedules to accommodate their own children. All I am saying is to put away any and every excuse and get involved; we owe it to our babies…

Knowledge is power…Educate and Empower…I pray this BOOK is a BLESSING TO ALL THOSE WHO READ THE WORDS ON THESE PAGES…It truly is written with L-O-V-E…Dedicated to Jeremy Christian Boyd, my son, who truly is the most AWESOME child I have ever KNOWN….A LOVE SO UNIMAGINABLE…AUTISM SPECTRUM DISORDER….SUPPORT THE CAUSE…

MEET THE BOYD FAMILY

Pictured from Left to Right

Shaundra Boyd, Morgan Boyd, Ashley Jeremy Boyd, and Jeremy Christian Boyd

Michael's Story

Table of Contents

Chapter I
Introduction
page 63

Chapter II
The Whirlwind
page 65

Chapter III
The Diagnosis
page 69

Chapter IV
Moving Onward and Upward
page 72

Chapter I
Introduction
Michael's Story

Finding out I was pregnant on February 14, 2001 was such an exciting occasion. During this time, I was dating my son's father and working towards completing my junior year in college. By the time I was 5 months pregnant, we made a decision that many young couples choose to make during times like this, which was to get married. Naturally in situations when there is a baby involved it seems that this is the "right thing to do", but hindsight, as they say, is always 20/20. During my pregnancy, I was extremely stressed and worried about ensuring that I was an adequate mother and wife, as well as asserting that I would finish college and not disappoint my parents. Each of these responsibilities weighed very heavily on me and I put forth effort towards each of them daily.

I gave birth to Michael Antonio Stewart Jr. on October 1, 2001. Initially I had the support of my husband as well as his family and my friends on this very important day. Unfortunately, my mother could not make it in until the following weekend, which was hard for me because we have a very close relationship. Having your mother there for the birth of your child, especially your first born, is a very important event, so part of me felt a bit empty, but when she did arrive I was excited that she was there to spend time with our new bundle of joy. Michael, who I refer to as "Mikey", was born with a clean bill of health, meaning he had no complications, as reported from our physician. As a new mother I did not foresee any problems as we began to care and nurture him throughout the beginning months of his life. I was excited to see him grow and change right before our eyes each day. It was a rewarding experience being a mother.

Chapter II
The Whirlwind
Michael's Story

After giving birth to Mikey, my life was a whirlwind as I balanced being a wife, mother and a college student. These responsibilities were all each extremely important to me and I felt that I gave each of them equal time to ensure that I was successful at them all. One very important thing that was missing during this time was a church home, therefore I went out to find one and thus, devoted my life to Christ. Now things seemed to be complete in my life. Emotional, spiritual, physical, and approaching financial wellbeing (finishing our degrees would bring us closer to this goal) all seemed to be in place and life seemed good. My husband also supported me as best he could by trying to be a good father, husband and man of God. However he was younger than I was and there was a part of him that felt as if he was still missing out on some things. In college, you are finally free to make your own decisions and my husband decided, after the fact, that being married with a child may not have been the best decision for him to make. He was a college athlete, pledging in a Greek fraternity and receiving more attention than he could handle from other women. Needless to say, this was a recipe for disaster.

When Mikey was around 11 months old; my husband woke up one morning, turned to me and said, "I don't love you, I never did. My son can stay, but you have two weeks to leave the home". Those words devastated me to the core of my soul. In my heart, I did not feel as though our marriage was over but it appeared as though my husband felt as if the things he was missing out on meant more to him than his family and so we separated. Although he mentioned that his son could stay but I needed to leave, I thought to myself, what mother would really walk away and leave her child, and so Mikey and I moved out of the home.

Although we were separated, we continued to remain involved and I constantly dealt with cheating, STD's, and lies, as well as being in verbal and physical altercations with other women. The final straw was when I found out my husband had gotten another woman pregnant. Even if I didn't want to give up on our marriage, it was necessary that I throw in the towel because his actions indicated that he had. I began now to focus heavily on finishing college and coming to the realization that I would be raising Mikey on my own. That was a hard realization to fathom because no wife ever marries to get divorced and decides to raise their child ALONE. It is unfortunate but it was the reality that I was faced with because of the man I had chosen to love. It is a hard to let go of someone that you thought would be your lifelong partner and that you have a precious son with, but it is even harder to continue to live a life that mirrors a whirlwind.

    My life became that much harder when Mikey turned 2 years old and began to cry more often than normal. He also stopped trying to verbally express himself to me. It was almost like had a relapse and it was very hard for him to understand and communicate his wants and needs to me. It was a very stressful time in my life as I was pressing myself to finish school. To be completely transparent, I had absolutely NO CLUE what was going on with my son. I was not sure where this behavior was coming from and why he had stopped communicating. The time went by so quickly and before I knew it I had finally finished pursuing my degree and Mikey was now 3 years. I made the decision then to move to Texas to be closer to my family. Family is the best support you can have and I needed that. All seemed to be progressing well in our lives during this time and then Mikey turned 4 years old and that's when the real whirlwind began.

**Chapter III
The Diagnosis
Michael's Story**

At 4 years old, Mikey was diagnosed with Pervasive Developmental Disorder- Not Otherwise Specified, also known as PDD-NOS. I can admit that I thought to myself what is PDD-NOS? During this time I was completely oblivious to what Autism was altogether, which resulted in my limited ability to develop appropriate coping skills to deal with Mikey's developmental concerns. What I did know was that my son could not verbalize himself and that he cried at almost anything. By this time, I had remarried and was with a man who completely adored my Mikey. He had two children of his own and together we became a wonderful blended family. After finding out about the diagnosis, my husband supported us and we became more sensitive to Mikey's emotional needs. When Mikey was around 4 ½, my husband and I were living with my parents. Every Sunday morning, we would leave the home around 5:00 a.m. to clean the church. I made sure that church was still an active part of my life because it was important to me. On one particular morning, we left Mikey, his 5-year-old son, and his 6-year-old daughter at home asleep on the floor. When we returned home, his son was laying on top of Mikey in an inappropriate sexual position. We were SHOCKED and as we separated the two boys and cried, we tried to gain a REAL understanding of what happened. I immediately gave Mikey a bath and as I did, I tried to get him to verbalize some type of details about this horrific event, but he struggled to explain anything about the experience he just encountered.

  Could you ever imagine that happening to your child? This is truly a parent's worst fear. Parents of non-verbal children on the Autism Spectrum live with this fear everyday. We fear that someone will violate or hurt our child and we will never know what happened because our child couldn't articulate what took place. More importantly, imagine what our child may feel inside as they go through experiences and cannot express themselves, especially those experiences that are so traumatic and detrimental that their emotional wellbeing is impacted.

  As time went on, my husband and I received counseling in order to attempt to move forward. My husband began to express resentment towards my son and stated how he did not like Mikey. He really couldn't explain why he felt that way but he also wasn't sure if he ever could like him again. I was baffled, and also hurt by the thought of this considering that his son was the one who put Mikey in the uncompromising position to began with. Then one day I saw a bruise on Mikey and found that it was my husband that put it on Mikey by hitting him and without a thought, I packed our bags and moved back to Georgia. Mikey was 7 years old by then and we were headed back to a place he had been before and about to encounter some new challenges that we didn't foresee. It almost seemed like a never-ending cycle of obstacles but my faith allowed me to remain tireless in my effort to seek happiness and stability for my family, Mikey and I.

Chapter IV
Moving Onward and Upward
Michael's Story

In Texas, Mikey was enrolled in the Crowley School District. This school district did a wonderful job devising goals and implementing them effortlessly with the help of the teachers, administrators, Mikey and myself. It wasn't until we moved back to Georgia when Mikey was 7 years old that we started to have issues in regards to school. Mikey was enrolled in a metropolitan Atlanta school district and our experience there not positive. The school was not well equipped for a child like Mikey. I felt as if he was the only child in the district diagnosed with Autism. Mikey was diagnosed with a mild form of ASD, which resulted in the school district placing him in a general educational setting because special education classes were filled with students who needed more one on one support. It was frustrating to deal with a district that seemed inept in regards to providing the services needed to ensure my son's educational success. Relying on my faith, I prayed and asked God for guidance and I received an answer that resulted in our move back to Texas so that Mikey could get the education he deserved and needed from the school district that I believed would truly have his best interest at heart.

    We have been back in Texas since 2008 and I can honestly say that I am overwhelming pleased with The Crowley Independent School District in Crowley, Texas. Mikey is in the 6th grade now and progressing well, making A's and B's. Each year the IEP team that comes together works cohesively to ensure that Mikey is achieving the goals that we set forth for him. Although I knew nothing about Autism before Mikey was diagnosed with it I devoted myself to conducting research through the Internet. I obtained a wealth of information that helps me support my son and his educational growth but even with the information found through Internet searches, I have only been able to utilize some of the recommendations on a trial and error basis. While my family has served as my troopers in regards to support, I still sought out support groups to get more information about PDD-NOS. However, what I found in those groups were that none of the children diagnosed with ASD were anything like my son. I have yet to meet another parent in my area with a child diagnosed with PDD-NOS and so I am still on a quest to find true support groups for parents with children similar to mine.

Financially we are grateful for all the services that we receive to assist Mikey, but I cannot deny the fact that I wish that there were more resources and funds available for us. Mikey receives both SSI and Medicaid and each of them are utilized to help provide his daily needs. Americans that have children diagnosed with ASD and earn higher incomes don't have to count their dollars like I do and can provide their children with medications, Gluten free diets, and other different approaches, as well as various types of schooling to help their child be successful. However, I live with the idea of knowing that without Medicaid, my son couldn't afford his monthly medication supply. I would love for Mikey to be a part of other schools and/or organizations that possibly could provide him more educational benefit, but my reality is that as a single mother, I can't afford those opportunities for him. While this may sound crazy to some of you, I have written letters to famous people trying to get some type of support for my son in hopes that he could have a chance at a better education. Oh how I wish I could afford to try the Gluten and Casein free diet without giving up my last dime. This is the world the world I am living in.

    I wish I could truly understand how to help Mikey beat

this diagnosis like Jenny McCarthy did (after reading her book I was truly inspired) but I know that it will never happen for me until I have the bank account that she does. If it were not for my faith in God, the government assistance, the support of my family and the church family, and the Crowley Independent School District, I honestly don't know how I would have made it raising Mikey. We are truly blessed and although we have a long road ahead, I will continue to look upward. The older Mikey gets, the easier it is to raise the wonderful child he is. The load becomes much lighter because he is maturing and coming into his own. I was told that I was the answered prayer for Mikey before he was even born. I thank GOD for entrusting me to raise such an amazing child.

Hoping this book reaches the masses…Michael and Trice!

MEET OUR FAMILY

Pictured from left to right
Lois Patrice Barks and Michael Stewart Jr.

The Yount's Report

Table of Contents

**Chapter I
The Beginning
page 78**

**Chapter II
Ignoring the Truth
page 81**

**Chapter III
The Truth Will Set You Free
page 87**

**Chapter IV
Our Life Today
page 90**

The Yount's Report
Chapter I
The Beginning

Our anticipated pregnancy with Brian was exciting yet low key in the beginning. I was a cashier supervisor at Target and later moved to becoming a shipping clerk/ Internet specialist for my parent's telephone company. It was an extremely low stress time in our lives during the beginning months of the pregnancy, but later a little apprehension grew as I began to wonder if I was feeling enough movement from the fetus. As time continued to progress I had to admit that I was becoming a bit worried. However, during our periodic visits to the doctor, Brian's heart rate was always normal, and since the doctor showed minimal worry about my concerns, I continued to move forward, assuring myself that everything was fine. Realistically, who ever wants to believe that something is wrong with their child? I surely didn't want to believe that Brian was having problems already so I tried not to think about it although subconsciously there lay a thought that there was some underlying issue.

The remainder of the pregnancy was up and down until it all came to a head on January 9, 2001. Our precious Brian was born in Houston, Texas and the delivery would prove to be a particularly traumatic one. I was sent to the hospital due to preeclampsia and was induced that night around 8:30 p.m. It was a rough night as the labor was extremely intense. We all were sleep deprived and I continued into labor until around 3:00 p.m. the next day. My water broke, and Brian's heart rate began to accelerate quickly. I knew things were going downhill because his movement inside was so frantic. The doctor's decided that it was necessary to do an emergency C-section and I was given a spinal epidural. This was a painful process, feeling like fireworks going down my spine. The pain was coupled with the doctor yelling intensely at me and I was unsure why. What I do remember is being in a confused state, crying frantically and lying there while they were trying to get Brian out, all while going in and out of consciousness due to exhaustion.

When the labor and delivery had all come to an end, I remember feeling a sense of relief because I thought that we had reached the end of a road of turmoil and pain. What I didn't know was that I was closing one chapter of chaos and would enter an entirely different chapter of confusion years later.

The Yount's Report
Chapter II
Ignoring the Truth

When we arrived home with Brian I was adamant about attempting to breastfeed him because I knew the positive results it could have on his health and wellness. I was so serious about it that I even hired a lactation specialist yet that still somehow proved to be unsuccessful. I pumped for a while, but made the decision to finally change to formula, which is a choice that I am still regretting to this day. I began to notice that Brian was becoming an irritable newborn, often being extremely sensitive to things such as the touch of cold wipes at diaper change time. He was also not getting as much sleep as other newborns would during their initial weeks home from the hospital. I wasn't sure why Brian was undergoing all of these changes and it really started to baffle me. Within three weeks of his arrival home, Brian developed reflux, which frightened me beyond belief. The sight of seeing him choking was one of the scariest things a mother could witness. I put him to sleep in his infant bed to keep him elevated at night hoping that this would somehow help. After

trying this for one night and being up until 5:00 a.m. the next morning, I decided to visit a specialist to get a remedy to this situation. We received a liquid form of Zantac
and was recommended to use the most sensitive formula on the market, which was Nutramigen. I could only afford the powered formula, and had to mix it with rice cereal, and cut open the nipples so that the formula could get through them. It was an absolute, huge mess! He developed colic,
which became even more frustrating.

    I managed to maintain my job, but Brian had to come to work with me. He continued to not get rest and I was falling into a life that was more stressful than I could have every anticipated. By 9 months Brian was sitting up and crawling and by 11 months he was walking and then running all over the house. He was always on the go and things seemed normal for a change.

    My parents would babysit him so we could go out on date nights. When we would return to get him, he wouldn't look at us for sometime, almost like he was furious that we had left him. He never seemed upset when we left him, only when we returned and I have never seen a child do this before. Around 10 months, it was time for Brian to go to

82

day care although I never wanted him to because I worked in one before and could take care of our son myself. He was sick every two weeks and had multiple ear infections that required him to take antibiotics every two weeks. The funny thing about Brian was that he didn't like to be held unless he was sick and weirdly enough that become our indication that a sickness was approaching. If he woke up in the middle of the night and wanted to be held then that was my sign that he was sick. This lasted for a few months and I made the decision that I needed to stay home with our son. After this, Brian quit getting ear infections but continued to get his immunizations as scheduled. However when seeing his doctor, we also found out that there was still fluid building in his ears. Although they told us that there was no infection we found out later that his hearing and speech were being affected and we became extremely concerned.

    We decided at this time to move to Georgia and by now Brian was almost 18 months old. It really upset him when we packed up to move. The sight of the boxes made him cry and once again I struggled to understand why. I also began to notice other weird things that were taking place that caught my attention. He became fascinated with watching ceiling fans.

Then I remember catching him at naptime smearing his feces all over his crib. I had never heard of a child doing this before. I had younger siblings in my house growing up and none of my childhood memories ever brought back these kinds of activities to mind. Nothing seemed right to me at all and it was very confusing to me. Little did I know at that time, that it was the beginning of a chain of events that would lead to something that we never saw coming.

Brian didn't communicate much and the most he would say was mama and dada. He used my hand to physically lead me to what he wanted. For example, if he wanted something to drink, he would lead my hand to the cup to get him what he needed. He would cry for everything else. I got to where I would just read the cries to figure it out. He was an extremely puzzling child.

On August 31, 2002, we moved in with my in-laws. Brian was such an active child, constantly getting into all of their things, which forced them to baby proof their house. In my opinion this caused a lot of resentment because they were required to put up baby gates to close off the kitchen and their coffee table in the attic, which they had no desire to do. Everything seemed so out of control and anything that happened was blamed on our son. I know it wasn't easy to have him around, but I had no idea why things were becoming so strained in our relationship with them. When Brian turned two years old, we took him to the doctor because I had a sense that there was something wrong with his development. The pediatrician told us that as long as he was pointing to what he needed that he was fine and that boys take longer to develop than girls do. His hearing was not checked at this appointment and because I was a mother who wanted to believe that everything was ok, I accepted what was told to me.

  We eventually moved out of the in laws house because it wasn't an ideal situation for any of us. There was a lot of damage done to that relationship that still has not been restored. We moved to another part of town and by this time I was ready to go back to work. I found work at a daycare that was close to where my husband worked so that we could use our one car to get us all to work. It was a very stressful job. Within a couple of months of starting, Brian's daycare teacher informed us that she thought he was developmentally delayed and cited examples of why she felt this way. She referred us to the Babies Can't Wait Program. I was in complete shock and cried the entire weekend. I didn't know what to think and I took out photo albums to look at Brian's baby pictures. There were many that told me a story that I had never noticed before. In many of the photos Brian had blank expressions and awkward facial expressions. His crawling was awkward in pictures as well because his feet never touched the floor. It is funny that pictures were telling us a story that we couldn't see in person or could it had been that we just that didn't want to see it. Denial is a scary place to be and it can have you look past even the most obvious things.

Chapter III
The Yount's Report
The Truth Will Set You Free

When Brian was almost three years old he was still not talking, could not use a spoon, and would cry for no apparent reason. It would take him hours to get to sleep at night and life for me had become unmanageable. As a mother, I never realized there could be such a problem. I became angry and cried a lot, even in front of Brian, who showed little empathy, and would even laugh at me. I went to the Internet to do some research because I had gotten to a point where I needed some real answers. I thought he might have Attention Deficit Disorder because I recalled being scattered when I was pregnant with him. I looked at the signs from the Internet, but it didn't remind me very much of Brian. Then I reviewed the warning signs of Autism. I got a gut wrenching feeling after seeing this list. I immediately began to cry. I couldn't believe it but I suspected there was more to this than him not being to communicate effectively. I contacted Babies Can't Wait and they completed a thorough assessment. The results indicated that he was functioning at 18 months in regards to his fine motor development and 14 months in the expressive communications category. Afterwards, I observed a 14 month old and that was a heart breaking experience to make that comparison to my own 3-year-old son.

    We decided to move forward with speech services through the school system that tested Brian's hearing and determined that the fluid build up made it hard for him to hear and was most likely affecting his speech. We took him to a pediatrician and it was decided that Brian needed tubes in his ears. We got them for him and then Brian began to receive services. I then went into research mode for Autism and found that I saw a lot of myself in the information that I located and even some of my husband's traits as well. It helped me to understand some of my own difficulties growing up.
It became more difficult for us as Brian's behavior continued to accelerate. He took off his clothes and refused to wear socks and shoes. He would love the swing, but other days he wanted nothing to do with it. He put woodchips in his mouth and often times would run away from me. He continued to smear his feces all over his bedroom. He jumped out of his bedroom window. Thank goodness his room was on the first floor! He pulled the fire alarm at my job at the end of the day. There

were times where I was horrified and embarrassed. It became even more difficult for me because people around me thought I was wrong and I didn't understand why. I could see it as plain as day now and how would anyone else know my son better than me? Each and every little quirk that I observed on a daily basis was confirmation of the diagnosis for me. He was lining up toys, had absolutely no fear and felt no pain, made little or no eye contact most times, didn't sleep, was often irritable, and lacked communication skills. His facial expressions didn't match his emotions.

      Brian didn't receive a diagnosis from the school system until he was 5 years old. The evaluation process consisted of me answering numerous questions that looked familiar to me because I had seen them from the Autism/ADHD checklists. When I met with the school psychologist to finally receive the evaluation, she informed me that Brian's diagnosis was ASD and for me, this was validation at best. I had been alone for two years, knowing the truth and having no one else believe what I had already confirmed through my own research.

Chapter IV
The Yount's Report
Our Life Today

When I suspected Brian had Autism at 3 years old, I grieved the loss of the dream of having a normal child. It took me a very long time to stop mourning that loss. The one true thing that brought me out of my depression was the idea of knowing that he was a happy child with a good life. Receiving the official diagnosis of Autism helped my husband and I to come together. By the time we received the diagnosis Brian was already enrolled in school and receiving special education transportation and doing particularly well and I know that this was because of the effort and work that I put in at home to understand and learn about this disability.

I continue to read and research what I can on the Internet to learn as much as I can about ASD to assist my son as he develops and grows to be the intelligent and well rounded young man he is today. I also participate in online support groups because I think it is important not to feel alone in this journey as parents of children who have been diagnosed with this disability. There are many times when I feel like my whole life is about Autism. I read something about it everyday from online boards or websites and get validation from hearing others struggles and victories with this multi faceted diagnosis. Support is critical, in my opinion, for parents of children with ASD because it helps to hear from other individuals that share similar experiences.

Reflecting on my life now as a housewife and full time mother, I am comfortable with where I am and being able to be available for Brian when necessary. He has the consistency he craves and the love he needs. However, financially I do sometimes wish we could afford to send him to a private school that specializes in Autism to allow him the opportunity to get instruction from teachers that are more adequately trained to support students with ASD. For my family, however, this type of schooling is not in our budget as can be expected for many families in similar financial situations. However, we do the best we can to work to support Brian's IEP goals/objectives. Some of the biggest challenges we face now are getting him to cooperate with those things that are best for him such as seeing the psychiatrist, and taking medication. It has been so hard to have to put him on medication, and we have faced a lot of criticisms for that decision. Breaks from school are also particularly trying for him as well, but as long as we take the time to discuss the expectations then it seems to help most of the time. My husband has been supportive throughout this process and I can always go to him for feedback on suggestions for improvements or to discuss what observations he has noticed in our son. With my decision to become a stay at home mother, there has been less sickness and chaos in our home. The consistency has been fantastic for the whole family!

While I never anticipated this to be our life, Brian truly is a loving and caring child that has two parents that will never give up on providing him with the best life possible. Autism Spectrum Disorder is a disability that has impacted our life profoundly but it will never impact the amount of love in our hearts for our son that is as precious to us now as he was the day he was born. We will forever be grateful to be blessed with the opportunity to parent such an AWESOME child. The number one thing Brian has taught us was unconditional love.

Thank you for allowing us the opportunity to share our story…The Yount's

Meet the Yount Family

Pictured from Left to Right
Brian C. Yount, Shiela A. Yount, Brian S. Yount, and Sharlet Yount

The Praylo Portrayal

Table of Contents

Chapter I
The Beginning
page 95

Chapter II
Piecing it Together
page 98

Chapter II
The Diagnosis
page 102

Chapter IV
Destini's Schooling
page 106

Chapter V
Summing It all UP
page 112

The Praylo Portrayal
Chapter I
The Beginning

Life during my pregnancy was an absolute breeze. I was free of the morning sickness and aches and pains that people mentioned I might feel because of this small stature of mine. I found out we were pregnant in May of 2002 and it was one of the most exciting times in our lives. This little life inside of me would definitely put a stop to my on the go life, but I was ok with accepting the new settled down lifestyle. I worked until about 7 months into the pregnancy and as months went by and I became a much larger Lisa, I started feeling like a real mother, developing those true motherly instincts and emotions, being protective of our little bundle of joy that was soon to arrive.

The night before Destini's unexpected arrival we were at the hospital visiting my father-in-law. Afterwards we decided to have dinner at a wonderful restaurant. I remember eating an unusual amount of food that night but being with family allowed us an opportunity to laugh and have fun in spite of the difficult situation that was happening with my father-in-law. What we weren't aware of was the fact that Destini had a plan to arrive much sooner than expected. The next day, on January 12, 2003, as we prepared to watch the Atlanta vs. Tampa Bay football game, I began to feel extremely uncomfortable. I felt unusual pains but I chalked it up to being greedy the night before at dinner. I was constipated and decided to take a warm bath, but because the water wouldn't get hot fast enough, I decided to take a nap instead. What I remember next was being rushed down the highway towards Candler Hospital. Being wheeled into my hospital room, I demanded to have to have the football game turned on, despite all of the pain I was in. I am an avid football fan so not many people were surprised by request.

    Simultaneously my husband comforted me while shouting at the television about touchdowns and fumbled balls. After receiving my epidural because Destini was ready to make a touchdown of her own, I felt awesome and was ready to conquer the world. When it was time to push, it didn't take long at all for Destini to enter into the world! Three or four pushes and our beautiful baby girl had arrived. Destini Marie Praylo, 7lbs 8oz, was quiet as ever and looked around ever so subtly. Then I heard her cry and it was the best yelp I had ever heard. Family and friends started to arrive to see our angel and life all seemed so normal. Never did we have a clue what the future would hold for our precious angel. She would have to endure several hardships in her life at an early age but it wouldn't be anything that together we couldn't overcome!

The Praylo Portrayal
Chapter II
Piecing It Together

Our life after the delivery was busy. I had a baby girl who was breastfed and loved it! I was a stay at home mom and my husband was always on the go with work. I had consistent days of one on one time with my angel and that is what I loved the most. The looks and stares as I read to her turned into smiles and giggles. Family was available but everyone had their own lives and I was too proud to ask for help. I went through sleep deprivation sometimes and no one knew the issues I experienced. Wanting to be superwoman had me seeing walls and objects move while I was standing still, but I made it through. Months went by and I remember seeing Destini scooting in her crib around 4 months and I was shocked. Babies aren't supposed to be this advanced I thought to myself but as my grandmother would say, "Watch out, she's trying to move out the way for another one".

As time progressed she began to roll over, scoot, and make cooing sounds. Destini was a very clingy baby and didn't want to be held by anyone but mom or dad. Even though she knew the faces of her grandmother and grandfather she would still cry. But doesn't every child that's at home with its mother every day do the same thing? That's what I believed and categorized it as a normal occurrence. We sat at home singing and reading stories, making animal sounds and doing fun children activities and Destini really enjoyed those things. She started crawling at 7 months and was walking a little shortly after her first birthday. Reaching for a donut is when she took her first steps, how likely is that!

She was a very happy child and as she got older she began to respond to her name and play with other kids like any other child her age. Right before Destini turned two, my husband and I made a big decision to take a job offer in Chattanooga, TN. In hindsight, I can't imagine making the same decision again, one that would take us away from our family, but we did. We moved in 2004 and there was absolutely no family around. Things were brand new for us, but Destini was still thriving and doing new things every day. We found a nice daycare for her and I began to work again. Leaving her at first was very hard for both of us, but we eventually got used to it. They loved her so much and took care of her like their own and I had no worries.

At the top of the list of things to do in a new city was to find a new physician. I searched and searched until I found one that I thought was a great fit for our family. She had her first appointment and it required updating her immunization because she was now in daycare and this was a requirement. Following the immunization schedule was all that I knew to prevent the spread of various diseases, therefore we followed the recommendations and that was the end of it, so we figured. Within a month my daughter started acting differently. We began to notice that when we called her name she was no longer responding. Then at dinnertime, she would want to take her food and sit under the table to eat. The daycare also started to communicate with us about a decline in her social skills. Destini was shutting down. Everything that we once knew of her started to fade away. What was happening? As parents you start to think: What is wrong with my child? What could have caused these changes so quickly? Why is this happening to her? Is there something that we did? I thought it was the quick move we made to another state and how she was no longer seeing the familiar faces of the people that cared about her the most. The daycare had a professional come in from Early Intervention to provide individualized support for Destini and a week later I took her to a physician to get more definitive answers.

Our ride to the physician's office was a quiet one. As a mother I was sensing and feeling things with no real justification for why. When we arrived to the physician, they performed several tests and asked a myriad of questions. I was in a confused state and anticipated the answers to why my child was no longer responding and behaving the way she once did. Then I heard a word I've never heard before …AUTISM. Autism? What exactly was this term and what do we need to do to fix it? After hearing what impact it could have on Destini's development, my heart stopped and I stood there thinking, what are we going to do? I wanted to do any and everything in my power to make her better. As parents we always hope that it is not our child, but the reality of this situation is that anyone's child could be affected by this disability…..ANYONE!

The Praylo Portrayal
Chapter III
The Diagnosis

I went home and researched the term Autism for myself because I refused to accept all of what the doctor had just said to me. We immediately removed Destini from the daycare she was currently enrolled in and placed her in another program where she could receive one on one services directed towards her social and communication skills. Before long she started experiencing meltdowns and outbursts. Indeed this was a time where I needed support and I couldn't allow my pride to get in the way. Don't get me wrong, my husband was extremely supportive, but he worked so many hours that when he came home, the day's events were almost at there end. We had to do something and we had to make a decision quickly, therefore we decided to move back to Savannah, GA. We had to go back home.

Within a month we were back home and arranging appointments with Destini's old doctor. Once again similar tests were completed that resulted in a diagnosis of ASD, Autism Spectrum Disorder. Hearing it this time around had very little impact on me, but getting a written report as an official diagnosis was powerful. The official diagnosis started to significantly impact our life in a great way and I knew that I had to do everything in my power to get my child back. Her doctor immediately suggested medication and I believed that this recommendation would be the fix. Destini was prescribed Risperdal and I immediately begin to see side effects with this medication. She began to gain weight quickly and started to refuse to do many of the activities she used to love to participate in. She also started to make mumbling noises and develop imaginary friends on her hands that she spent a lot of time with. She began to pull her hair out and eat it, fixate on cheese, and all the beginning symptoms of her ASD were progressively getting worse.

    Her dad was having a difficult time grasping the concept of what was taking place with his daughter. It was hard to accept that the baby girl that he adored had changed so drastically. He loved her so much and enjoyed singing to her and seeing that beautiful smile but she seemed so different now. Destini is the splitting image of her father, but because he had been absent due to work, it was difficult for him to understand some of the things that she had been going through.

I vividly remember taking Destini to the playground one day and watching her play in her own small space as if there were no other children around. Other children were running around, laughing and playing, interacting with one another and Destini acted as if they didn't even exist. We also would often find ourselves driving around in the car and even in the house playing music because she enjoyed hearing music so much. I would always hear humming in the back of the car as we rode, but never words uttered to go along with the songs. We prayed and prayed that one day we would hear her voice and truly God is a God that answers prayers.

Riding in the car one day listening to Mary J. Blige's, "Just Fine", a song she would always bobbed her head to, Destini decided to echo the words behind me. I looked back and the most beautiful sound was coming from her lips. I was shocked and before I knew it, I screamed in excitement, "Oh my God, is that you Destini?" She began to smile and continued on singing. Tears flowed down my face and I thanked God again and again for answering our prayers. I went to the store and brought that CD for Destini and I am not at all surprised that she still listens to it today.

Once the talking began it has never ceased. She started speaking more words and then sentences and making request and that's when something hit me. I truly imbedded in my head a "not my child" attitude. The "not my child" attitude means that I truly began to believe that my child CAN do any and every other thing any other child CAN DO despite the disability and diagnosis she received. We were going to make sure that this would happen for Destini. I became this superwoman that initiated a push in Destini that would ensure that she would excel to unbelievable heights. If it can be done, she would do it!

The Praylo Portrayal
Chapter IV
Destini's Schooling

By now, Destini was 4 years old, in Pre-Kindergarten and was so excited! I was unaware of the responsibilities that would come along with having her enrolled in a special needs program in a public school setting. Her first school experience opened with tantrums, biting, and scratching, all of which we believed stemmed from the fear and anxiety of being in a new environment. As a parent, I had to admit that I was fearful a little myself. IEP's, meetings, teachers, and paraprofessionals were all a bit overwhelming. What helped me make it through the school year was remembering the commitment I made to Destini and the superwoman "S" that I wore on my chest for my daughter.

Destini was still taking her prescribed Risperdal at this time and we continued to see her weight fluctuate and the other adverse affects that had resulted from taking this medication and ultimately we made the decision to take her off. I never wanted her to be dependent on medication anyway and in order to know if she could function normally without medication, we needed to see how she would behave off of it and that is what we did.

Destini stayed at one school for two years and became familiar with the teachers and the academic program. Her grandmother was one of the bus drivers for the school, which means she had the chance to see her often, giving Destini even more comfort while at school. I chose not to let her ride the school bus for her first two years of school but when she began to request to ride, I felt obligated to grant it to her because I believed she was ready and who was I to stop her. After Kindergarten they moved the program she was attending to a different school with a different teacher and paraprofessional. This new school was all the way across town and I had to provide the transportation back and forth for her daily. By this time, we were pregnant again, with twins, and the stress of staying involved and being pregnant, presented quite a task, but it was done and with love. I loved this school because they made Destini feel so welcomed and involved her in so many meaningful activities. She received speech therapy and was in a special needs classroom with one on one instruction where the teachers updated me frequently on her progress. Not only was she communicating but she began to count, learn all her colors, and forming sentences.

    The program now was being moved to another school and we felt like we were on yet another merry go round ride. Destini was now in the 2nd grade and was riding the school bus, which didn't pose a concern to me by now because I had built close relationships with the bus drivers and knew them fairly well. Destini was now attending a school that was the complete opposite of the previous school she attended. We felt unwelcomed and they didn't want to include the special needs children in any additional activities outside the classroom. The twins had arrived by this time and kept us very busy, but I refused to allow that to be an excuse why I was not actively involved at Destini's school. I continued to ensure that Destini be included in as many activities as possible. I was there so often that I remember hearing the office staff say, "There is Mrs. Praylo again, she stays up here, it would be nice if the other parents were this involved". They knew me quite well and I made it my business to know what was taking place at all times. I ensured that the services indicated on Destini's IEP were, in fact, being implemented and that she was being treated appropriately.

As she started to get adjusted to the new school, teachers, and her surroundings, another bombshell occurred. They moved the program yet again and this time it happened only two weeks into the academic school year. I was livid because the notice was so short and they didn't think about the student's at all in their decision to make this abrupt move. The positive side to this move was that her teacher and paraprofessional were able to transition along with her; thus the move went more smoothly than anticipated. The new school location was more welcoming and although the school was farther out than the other schools had been before, I was ultimately pleased with the decision.

I was back at work, Destini was in school, and the twins were in daycare. During this time in Destini's schooling something wonderful truly began to happen for her. She began to climb to new heights. She was now in inclusion, where she spent time in her special education class, but was now also included in the regular 2nd grade classroom. When this occurred she continued to soar. She was around students her age, going to music and science classes with them daily. She was also included in Christmas programs and she was excited to be included with her classmates. In 3rd year, Destini continued to thrive and even become popular in school. Walking with her down the hall one day in school, I remember kids from Kindergarten to 5th grade speaking to her and that really made her feel good. She started to blossom into this young lady that I almost didn't recognize. It seemed to happen so fast. This was the year of independence for her. She wanted to do things all on her own with no assistance and I didn't stop her. She was putting up her own clothes and preparing her own lunches for school. She also wanted to walk to the bus stop alone but I wasn't going to allow that to happen. She also started playing softball this year and socializing with teammates. She was turning out to be much like her mother, very athletic. This opened up another door for her to accomplish different goals and she did just that.

Destini's 4th grade year has been, by far, the best year yet. During this year we began to talk about middle school and college and this conversation ignited a fire in her that I have never seen. She worked extremely hard this year completing all her homework assignments projects, reading chapter books, and completing all subject area work especially science. For the first time she made the HONOR ROLL. That boosted her confidence so much that she made that a goal for every report card!

    Some people may think that I am extremely hard on her but that's isn't at all how I see it. It is about being strict and setting expectations and goals because that's what parents are supposed to do. I am not going to sell my daughter short because she has a disability. I am supposed to push her to ensure that she reaches her fullest potential and that is exactly what I am doing. Odds are stacked against her already but we aren't going to allow that to stop her from pursuing every dream; wouldn't you do the same for your child?

    My family is so blessed to have received the angel that we were given. She has shown us patience, love, and that no matter what the situation is, Christ will strengthen you and guide you through it. I stated in the beginning of our story that we would never allow this disability to prevent our baby from achieving her dreams and it hasn't yet and never will it.

The Praylo Portrayal
Chapter V
Summing It All Up

    While initially I had no clue what Autism was, I am more knowledgeable now that I have conducted research online. The key to researching is to ensure that you find reputable sites that are providing researched based information from reliable sources. I also received information from doctors because they have worked with various children with Autism and are experts in the field. Parents must educate themselves not only about the disability itself but also about the various medications that are typically prescribed by doctors and the potential side effects they have on our children. Talking to other parents about your experiences is a great source of support because sharing information and knowledge with people who understand can potentially help you gain more insight and awareness about the disability.

    While Destini has been involved in many extracurricular activities, financially many special needs summer camps that I would love for her to attend have astronomical prices if assistance is not available to cover the cost of the fee. Because middle class families don't have the income that would allow them to send their child to these camps, we are forced to send them to less specialized facilities or keep them at home, which serves little or minimal benefit to them. Destini is extremely active in many sports, and although some parents of children with ASD stay away from the sports arena, we have found that playing sports has truly brought her personality out. She plays softball for the Port Wentworth, GA Patriots now and has been for 2 years in the right outfield position. Her coaches are absolutely amazing and extremely patient with her. Her teammates help bring out the best in her and we love that they understand her for who she truly is. It would be my hope that more assistance could be provided for middle class families to support our children since often times we are the class of families left to suffer because our income does not qualify us at all for any services. It puts our children at a disadvantage in some aspects. The wonderful thing is that I work with my daughter to support her educational goals on a daily basis; can the same be said for other children as well?

  As we close this chapter, we wouldn't be who we are without paying homage to our family for the support they have given us throughout the years. They have supported Destini and our entire family as we have experienced the triumphs and trials to come to this understanding that we have now of what Autism Spectrum Disorder is and how it has and will continue to impact our lives.

I pray that this book reaches millions of people so that they can truly know and hear our story and that we impact someone's life in a profound way…THE PRAYLO FAMILY!!!

MEET THE PRAYLO FAMILY

Pictured from left to right

Destini Praylo, Sherlisa Praylo, Richard Praylo, and Jada and Jayden Praylo

My Precious Chloe

Table of Contents

Chapter I
The Start of It All
page 117

Chapter II
From This…
page 120

Chapter III
To What? (The Diagnosis)
page 123

Chapter IV
Living Our Life Today
page 126

Chapter I
The Start of It All
My Precious Chloe

My pregnancy with Chloe was considered high risk. Any mother that has been grouped into this category during their pregnancy knows all that comes along with it. I fell into this group because I was diagnosed with both high blood pressure and gestational diabetes; needless to say, I was truly high risk and was at a pivotal point during my life. Regardless of all of these things going on, I maintained an excitement about the upcoming birth of my beautiful baby girl, Chloe, and that was something, no health condition could take away.

During this time, I was working as a customer service manager at Kroger and although I was in this high-risk category, I managed to maintain this job even while being sick for the first five months of the pregnancy. I also attended Georgia State University as a student working to pursue a degree in Early Childhood Education. A few months before delivering Chloe, I left Kroger and became a substitute teacher in a metropolitan Atlanta school district. I enjoyed this job because it prepared me for my career in early childhood education and also for becoming a parent (killing two birds with one stone so to speak).

The labor and delivery was very long, lasting for two arduous days. On day two of being in the hospital and at the time of actually delivering Chloe, she experienced some very serious complications. Her skin turned from light to a dark purplish color. I was in complete awe of what I was seeing! I was experiencing an array of emotions with confusion being at the forefront. In your mind you truly believe that everything will run so smoothly and that you'll leave the hospital after delivering a healthy baby without any worries. That wasn't in the plans for us. The doctor explained to me that Chloe had breathing complications, which caused her to ultimately, have a seizure. A seizure? My newborn? Wow! That is all I could think and I was terrified that my newborn daughter had undergone that type of trauma already. Motherhood was new to me and I wasn't ready to deal with this so soon, but it was my reality and I had to take it as it came. I wasn't giving up at all because my Chloe needed me to be strong and that is exactly what I was for her.

After having the seizure, Chloe was required to stay in the hospital for a couple of weeks and I was there by her side every step of the way. It is what every mother would do for her child and I was no different. I was ready for us to finally be released and eventually that time came. I was excited for the time to come to take my Chloe home and it had finally arrived.

Chapter II
From This...
My Precious Chloe

Once Chloe arrived home, I had to continue to take her back and forth to various doctor's to have her tested. She was also required to take seizure medication for a while, which was very stressful for me as a parent of a newborn baby. I was stressed because I was uncertain as to how this medication was making my child feel because clearly she was unable to communicate this information to me. I was also unaware of the potential side effects this medicine could cause to her brain. This was a serious matter to me and I was apprehensive and as a parent that was serious about my child's health and wellbeing, and I should be.

Chloe began to grow and develop as other newborns did her age and as time began to fly, weeks were turning into months, and then months into years. As Chloe got older, around 2 years old, I began to notice a lot of differences in her compared to other kids her age. She would say words but she wasn't forming short sentences. She appeared very timid and shy around other people. She enjoyed playing with others but she would be just as happy to play by herself, as long as she had Barbie dolls or movies to watch.

By 3 years old I made the referral myself for Chloe. At this age, she attended a popular childcare facility in South Fulton County. I wasn't one of those parents that were in denial about my child. I knew that she was experiencing some developmental delays and I know this was partly because of my education in the education field. I was sure that Chloe was SDD, meaning Significantly Developmentally Delayed, and I only needed an expert to validate that information. After the referral, the testing concluded that there were indeed, learning and language difficulties as well as, attention deficits, that Chloe was experiencing. At that point, it was obvious that she had a SLD (Specific Learning Disability and ADHD (Attention Deficit/Hyperactivity Disorder) along with language development issues; however at this age, they are only required to diagnosis it as SDD.

After the required testing and evaluations, Chloe was placed in Special Needs Kindergarten this school year and only left the classroom for lunchtime. Chloe's first grade year, however was a bit different, because she was placed in a regular homeroom class and her special education teacher would come to pick her up during academic times. Chloe would return to the general education setting for her specials classes and lunch. This type of learning placement continued for her first and second grade academic school year. By the close of her second grade year, Chloe was labeled as SLD/ADHD as I knew she would be, after the transition from SDD.

Chapter III
To What? (The Diagnosis)
My Precious Chloe

When Chloe entered 3rd grade she was showing little academic improvement and I was extremely concerned. Chloe was being co-taught for Social Studies/Science, which was great exposure for her, but it was still too overwhelming for her learning style. This was when I began to notice that she had similar traits to many of the students with Autism Spectrum Disorder that I worked with in my own classroom. No other professionals that worked with Chloe had ever brought this to my attention, so I thought I maybe over thinking things, but it became clear that I wasn't.

By the close of the 2012-203 school year, we all realized that my concerns were accurate and Chloe should be on the Autism Spectrum. At her IEP meeting in April 2013, Chloe was officially diagnosed with ASD as her primary disability. When I heard the news, I was a little saddened but not at all surprised. Things changed very little for my family, but I made it a point to educate family members and close friends about the challenges Chloe faced day in and day out with this disability. They were beginning to understand why she was afraid to use the restroom alone, why she wasn't a fan of big crowds, and why she often would stand still and squeeze her legs tight together. They were also beginning to grasp why she would always assume people were looking at her, why she often stared at people really hard, or why she wasn't as affectionate as she should be at times. Lastly they were able to fathom even why she constantly talked to herself, why she has emotional break-downs at times, why she doesn't focus on her school work, and why she seemed as if she didn't understand different emotions on people's faces. I know this seems like so many different types of behaviors, but for mothers of children with Autism they can relate and they know exactly what all this means. It is a lot and it can be overwhelming when you don't know what you are looking at, but we all work through them everyday with our beautiful children and we still walk away each night, and wake up each morning ready to do it all over AGAIN.

   Sometimes I can shed tears about what is going on and when I do, Chloe will laugh and then all of a sudden she gets very upset. Sometimes so upset that she would begin to pull her hair bows out of her hair. During Christmas programs, she would know her speech with perfection, but the cameras, bright lights, and large crowds would cause her to stand still and appear as if she wanted to head for the first door in sight. Can you IMAGINE what Chloe must feel daily as she is trying to understand how to process and take all of this in? Autism Spectrum Disorder is a challenging disability for those on the outside looking in to comprehend, but it is even more difficult for the one who has to experience it day in and day out, with the looks and stares, and glares, and turned up noses, and laughs, from people who are too ignorant to know what they are truly seeing. As a parent, I'm proud of my Chloe because she has made great strides in the social skill arena and she will be able to function as a citizen in society regardless of the label she has received. However, there are many children diagnosed with ASD who aren't as fortunate as Chloe, but they still deserve your respect. All it takes from you is to get educated about this profound disability that affects so many!

Chapter IV
Living Our Life Today
My Precious Chloe

The ups and downs in the public school system have me strongly considering The Bedford School for students with Autism in the near future. Public school, in my opinion, isn't able to fully cater to Chloe's learning needs. This is a constant that I think most parents feel in regards to their special needs students that attend school in the public education sector. While I believe that most teachers are committed to the students in their classroom, I want to ensure that Chloe has the ability to have instruction in a specialized setting that is conducive to her exceptionality. Public school system settings do not offer that luxury for a variety of reasons.

My knowledge and experience with this unique disability comes from my own education and experience, as a special needs educator. I was equipped with a wealth of knowledge and resources about Autism and thus I was able to apply that to my own life with my child. I am always eager to learn more about the disability and while this diagnosis has proven to be a costly one, it will never hinder me from giving her the best of everything.

Chloe has needed tutorial services, activity outlets, and sensory equipment, which are extremely expensive, and I haven't hesitated to sacrifice to provide it for her. As time has passed, I have managed to secure medical and financial resources to assist me with this laundry list of needs to help Chloe meet her educational goals. As a middle class mom working to provide for my children, the Bedford schooling as well as other activities, often times are more costly than I can afford, but that will never stop me from ensuring that she is afforded the best opportunities available to her. Chloe is a blessing and truly a special child and I am excited to share our story with you in this amazing book.

Thank you for taking the time to read and understand about our lives. CHLOE is truly AWESOME in her OWN RIGHT!

Jillian Brown

Meet Our Family

Pictured from left to right
Chloe Fuller, Rilei Fuller, and Jillian Brown

References

Bogin, J., Sullivan, L., Rogers, S., & Stabel. A. (2010). *Steps for implementation: Discrete trial training.* Sacramento, CA: The National Professional Development Center on Autism Spectrum Disorders, The M.I.N.D. Institute, The University of California at Davis School of Medicine.

THANK YOU FROM THE AUTHOR

Thank you for taking the time out to read the pages of this book. Autism Spectrum Disorder is a unique disability that affects millions of Americans. It is important for me to bring awareness to as many individuals as I can about this unique disability. EARLY INTERVENTION for children that may show signs of any developmental disability is the key to ensuring that they have the best outcomes overall.

RESOURCE LIST

1. http://www.autismspeaks.org

2. http://www.autism-society.org/living-with-autism/family-issues/

3. http://www.autisminspiration.com

4. http://www.autismcares.org/site/c.mqLOIYOBKlF/b.4745901/k.BD21/Home.htm

5. http://www.child-autism-parent-cafe.com/index.html

6. http://www.eparent.com

7. http://www.lincolntent.com/GFCF.html

8. http://www.dsm5.org/Documents/Autism%20Spectrum%20Disorder%20Fact%20S heet.pdf

9. http://www.autismasperger.net

10. http://autisminaction.com/parents.html

Made in United States
Orlando, FL
03 February 2024